How To Get Answers Every Time You Pray®... About Who You Are

A.D. Long

Published by Interfaith University in partnership with AMC.

ISBN:

DEDICATION

To all those seeking to understand your placement in life,
be encouraged! God is here and more than able to see
you through.

CONTENTS

INTRODUCTION

We all at some point or another have been on a quest in life to understand why we were born, who we are, and what we are to do with our lives. If you are still searching for the answers to these questions, this is a point where God can find you and help you through. The first thing to do when you find yourself searching is to look for God. Prayer is a great way to understand who we are. God, our Father, would know this best because He placed use in our bodies at the time we were born for a reason. God told Jeremiah "***Before I formed thee in the belly I knew thee... (Jere. 1:5)***." So, God would know who we are and what He intended for us to be before anyone else would know because before we were placed on this earth, our spirits resided in and with Him. He formed us, so we must consult Him to understand the details of who He shaped us to be.

CHAPTER 1:
YOUR QUEST SHOULD BEGIN IN PRAYER

Prayer is a great way to understand the intentions of God. It is through us communing with Him that we can get a concept of His intended will for us. It is like you and a friend. If you never converse with your friend and spend time with them, you will never know or understand their mind. So, prayer gives us that opportunity to commune with God so that we can understand His heart.

You are not alone. I have also found myself on this quest. Wondering why God placed me on this earth, who I was to be, and what I was to do with my life. I was once filled with uncertainty about who I was. Not sure or having any clue as to what I wanted to really do in life, just hoping to get an understanding one day. I have always enjoyed fashion and have worked as a fashion consultant and designer. And yes, I love what I do, but after the fashion shows, the compliments, and the hype, I would still sit to myself wondering who am I. The emptiness and void would scream louder than anything in my mind. It wasn't until I got a hold of the teaching from Dr. Hoffman on prayer and partnership that I was able to get a true understanding of my identity. I learned to pray and confess what God said in His word about me. After doing so, my perspective about who I was changed and I began to see what God said about me. The journey of finding my identity all started by getting into prayer and connecting with other believers. There is no other way to get an understanding of who you are without connecting with God and his people.

I am reminded of a woman named Lydia, who was also on this same quest. Here story can be found in the book of Acts chapter 16. She was a successful businesswoman who sold purple dyed cloth. Her occupation would be somewhat equivalent to someone in the fashion industry today. Those who sold this infamous purple dyed material were highly revered in their cities. Even with all the popularity and notoriety, Lydia still found herself on a search to know who she was. She let go of the customs of her hometown and began her search for God. She was found with other women on the riverside and there she met Apostle Paul. It was through pray and a divine connection, that God revealed to her who she was. She found her destiny and greater hope, but her journey started, once again, through prayer and connection with God's people.

This book reflects on the importance of yielding to God in prayer, agreement with the body of Christ, understanding God's will, impartation, confession, and understanding partnership. So, be encouraged! Because you too can receive answers every time you pray about who you are according to God's word.

CHAPTER 2:
WHAT IS AGREEMENT?

Your quest to understand who you are must start with agreement with other believers in the word. When you are in sync with the body of Christ, nothing can be restrained from you in prayer. *"Assuredly I say unto you, whatsoever you bind on earth shall be bound in heaven and whatsoever ye shall loose on earth shall be loosed in heaven. Again I say unto you that if two of you shall agree on earth as touching anything that they shall ask, it shall be done for them of my father which is in heaven."* **Matt. 18:18-19.** *"Can two walk together, except they be agreed?"*

Amos 3:3

To agree comes from the Greek word **sumphoneo (soom-foe-neh-oh) from sum-together and phoneo- to sound. Sumphoneo means *to sound together, to be in symphony, to be in accord, to be in harmony*.** Metaphorically, the word means to agree together in prayer. The verses above in Matthew 18:18-19 deal with the power that believers have to call heaven on earth. Let's look back at verse 18... **whatsoever**... you bind...**whatsoever** you loose, heaven will *agree* (when it's scripturally sound). When believers pray, results manifest. Oh that we would learn of the more than **60 categories of blessings** that Christ died for! The Bible commands us to "...forget not all of HIS benefits...".

I once read a survey that stated that 80% of people in church, who are called to be like God (our Father which is in heaven), are dying- spiritually, physically, mentally, socially, and yes, even financially. This should not be. We need to go back and recheck the definition of the word "saved". Saved from what? Sin? Well, if the sin is gone, we should realize that God does not do a half job and that Christ died to make us whole in our body, in our soul, and in our spirit. He came to bind up the brokenhearted, not to fix one part and leave the rest of you broken.

Never forget, Satan's job is to control you by unbelief in the atonement of Christ. So, the 80% do not pray because they reason what's the use in disciplining yourself and afflicting yourself to commune with a God that has no provision. This is the subconscious reason in the hearts of men and thus 80% of those approaching God through church attendance cannot experience the free flow of the blessings that God has so wondrously laid out for them! JESUS! HELP US! Therefore, we can't agree on what God says, for many times we don't know.

The Bible says in **Hosea 4:6** that God's people are destroyed, not because Satan is so powerful, not because they are to be so afflicted, broken, ragged, or pious, but we are destroyed for a lack of knowledge! It's time for us to learn the benefits of salvation in the fullness of the revealed knowledge of the scriptures. Begin to pray and give like never before, until our prayers reach heaven building a memorial before God as Cornelius did.

Then God will connect us with a Peter that has prepared himself through prayer for the glory of God. There will be an exchange of anointing and power that will fall on us as the Holy Ghost fell on Cornelius and his house and the miracles and benefits, we have read about will become an unmistakable, unquestionable reality!

When we understand where we fit in unity with His people, we will see the harmony we have with God and will truly see the power we possess. John 17:16-17, 20

CHAPTER 3:
PRAYER

Before we go any further let us define the word prayer or pray. We must reshape the incorrect persona of prayer. Prayer is not you doing all of the talking to God. Pray should be a mutual thing. It is you talking to God and God talking to you. Pray as explained by Jesus means in the Greek ***prosseuchomai*** (pros-yoo-khom-ahee). The word is progressive starting with the noun ***euche***, which is a prayer to God that includes ***making a vow***. The word expands to the verb ***euchomai***, a special term describing "an invocation, request or entreaty". Adding pros, in the direction of God, **prossechomai** becomes the most frequent word used for prayer.

The word invocation is where we will find the power of agreement. (Invocation, is the process of making requests or petitions.) In Genesis 11, the unity of the people caused God to take notice of what was going on at the Tower of Babel and come down to stop the work and confuse the languages. So, when we unify or exhibit unity, it causes God to show up. (His presence comes down). Look at it from the positive. After the Resurrection of

Jesus, he told his disciples to wait in Jerusalem for the promise of the Holy Spirit. So, as a result of unity, on the day of Pentecost, they were all together with one accord and God came down again (Acts Chapter 2)!

Unity at work directed toward God for anything whether negative or positive will get God's attention. Now we have unity- that is if you have been born again, you have the measure of unity that brings you into the family of God. The key is to learn from the Word of God how to work that unity for the positive, productive reasons God gave it to you! Unity is not enough being left alone; it must be activated in the direction toward God! So, when you unify with others in pursuit of understanding who you are, activate your unity together in God and you will receive what you ask of Him.

CHAPTER 4:
IT!

The prayers of believers sometimes go unanswered because they do not express to God what they are dealing with. Imaging your child coming to you in request for something but do not seem to articulate exactly what they want from you. You would probably ask them for more details but if they still are not saying exactly what IT is, you cannot really help them, can you? It is the same way with God. Our Father wants to help you with your inquiry, but you must express what IT is that you need from Him.

Now, let's deal with IT! One of the reasons many praying Christians have unanswered prayers is the IT! Some are praying for IT and IT does not come. Why? Because IT has to be not only in unity with a person on Earth, but it has to be loosed from heaven. The following process will get you anything you need (Philippians 4:19), want (Psalms 23), or desire from God (Psalms 37:4); for it is the Father's good pleasure to give you the kingdom!

1. Analyze the situation- Find out what your needs are, what your debts are, what your sickness is, or what the fear is about. Find out how much of what it is you need in order to sustain yourself, your family and the House of God! 2 Corinthians 13:5 says that we must ask of God to help us to know ourselves, so we are not asking amiss!

2. Research God's Remedy- Just as you

would ask your pharmacist or doctor which medication is best for a specific problem, ask the great Physician to show you in His written Word what the cure is. To get answers when you pray about who you are you must know exactly what God says about you in His word. So, ask God for His perspective, then search and research the Bible until you have allowed the Holy Spirit to convince you of the truth that Christ has redeemed you from the curse of the law (Galatians 3:13). Start by getting your notebook and write down every verse you see that says who you are in Christ.

3. Ask, Seek, Knock- Once you know the will of God based on scripture- not a prophet or any other person- but have found it in the Word of God, then He hastens his Word to perform it (Matthew 7:7)! This means it consistently persists in growing intensity and faith until the Master of the house gets up and grants your request! Simply requesting is not enough you must continue in prayer, continue to seek, continue to knock until you get a full understanding of who you are in God.

4. Partner- You may be saying "...I ask, I seek, I knock, but I still can't seem to get my breakthrough!" Then bring in the atomic bomb... partners. When it seems as though you have reached your faith limit- remember that there are other saints that have conquered this level of negative force and you have access to their faith through the power of agreement (James 5:14-16)! Look for someone who has overcome in the area you are weaker in. Notice the Bible says, "call for the Elders of the church". There are two principles here that should not be ignored:

a. Elder- means older, not necessarily in age, but maturity in the Lord! An elder is at least mature in the area that you are struggling with. Warning: if you have a problem or weakness, a prayer partner with the same weakness is not going to build you up; for he has not developed himself to the point that he is strong enough to bear your infirmity and his! Therefore, instead of agreeing with God, you begin to unite against God, and you get a Tower of Babel or a Tower of Confusion!

b. Remember that the binding and loosing power is connected to the CHURCH.

Make it a rule not to partner with anybody in prayer who is not firmly rooted in a local church! (At least not to get your deliverance!) It is fine to pray with a person who is not in church who understands that the focus of the prayer is for their edification mainly, but remember if you need strength, you must find strong prayer partners (Matthew 18:18-19). You may go as far as to say that you already have a prayer partner, but there is still a problem. In such a case, start at steps 1-4 and if all lines are clear, bring in another prayer partner and another and another until you have enough power in prayer to bind the strong man or negative force that is blocking your flow of blessing! Just make sure every prayer partner understands and has done the above things and can agree with you that this IT is the will of God and He wants you to have IT. Start building your prayer partnership today!

5. Praise and worship God in Faith and watch it manifest!

6. Separate from bad company, negative friends, bad teaching and preaching not in faith in God's total Word (I Corinthians 15:33).

7. If the enemy attacks you with doubt- do it again (Galatians 6:6).

The bottom line is your IT must line up with your prayer partner's level of faith and the will of the Father in Heaven. Well, how do we know the will of the Father? We must know, agree, and also pray according to the Word of Almighty God. If God says IT, bank on IT, agree with God! Say what God says and you will truly have whatsoever you say! Now what is your IT? Matthew 6:33 deals with seeking first righteousness and He will commence to dropping it on you!! How do you seek the kingdom?

1.) Watch and pray for opportunities to sow- finance, time, energy, and prayer into an anointed ministry that is spreading the Good News of THE KINGDOM OF GOD! A ministry with VISION.

2) Preach the Word- Witness to friends and neighbors. Give away tracts, good sound Christian books, tapes and videos. Get the gospel out any way you can in the Spirit of God. (Pray about it!!)

3) Put God first- Stop thinking of how much you can get from God and think about how much you can do for God's kingdom! You may require only a small crampy compact car for yourself, but the kingdom of God may call for a minivan to transport people to church. Pray until you find out what God wants you to have because that is your need. Your family may require only a two-bedroom house, but to help some Christian brother or sister, the kingdom may call for a five-bedroom home. Seek first the kingdom and His righteousness! It's time to get IT right because when you hunger and thirst to do right by helping others, you will be blessed and blessed and blessed. Well, should you run off and sow financial seed to everything asking and moving or looking like the kingdom? No!! Would you sow peas one or two or three to a field? No!! Because you would have to go to two or three different locations just to get started on a pot!!

The bottom line is to sow where:

a) God leads,

b) The ground is good,

c) The Gospel is being preached,

d) Souls are being saved, and

e) Christians are edified.

Do all of this under the anointing or the witness of the Holy Spirit! Pray. God will direct your path. What is IT? Let's touch and agree and it is done according to God's will.

CHAPTER 5:
GOD'S WILL

Another common issue that sometimes arises when dealing with prayer is "what do I say?" I do not know how to use the thee and thou words or don't have a hold lot to say off the top of my head. Let me tell you up front, prayer is not hard. Finding what to say to God during prayer is not hard, simply go to His word. God's word reveals His will for His people. Think of God's word as a will. What is a will? Well, when someone passes it shows the intent of that person for those who were a part of their family, their friends, etc. See, God's word shows His intents for you. It shows exactly what He wants you to have. So, when you delve into God's word you will find all sorts of promises and blessing that He has for His people. God wants us as his children to come to Him boldly and remind Him of what He said He would do for us or what He promised us. So, finding what to say in prayer is not hard, simply look in His word and remind Him of what He said He would do for you.

Reciting to God His word guarantees that you will get what you asked of Him. He will not withhold no good or beneficial thing from you if it is according to His word. You see that is why many believers do not receive answers to their prayer because they are not praying according to God's word or God's will. God is not a man that He should lie or the son of man that He should repent. If He said it in His word, He cannot take it back. If He did it for someone else, He has to do it for you too. His word will not and cannot change. So, if you have not yet seen answers to what you are believing God for, it's time that you take another look at His will.

We have already established that God's Word is his will. But let's dig deeper!! If you truly want to be blessed, you must allow God to speak to your heart about your need and to back it up with scripture. You must make that scripture and revealed Word from God your faith. That's right, the moment God makes a word alive in your spirit you have faith. Now! Hebrews 11:1 says, "Now faith!" Romans 10:17 tells us, faith comes by hearing and hearing by the Word of God.

Faith is trust and confidence in God's word. Through reading and understanding His word, you can build such confidence. You can proclaim His word back to Him until you see what He said come into fruition. We can miss out or don't see the promises of God simply because we fail to have faith in the face of trouble. Some saints of old refused their deliverance when they knew God could get them out of their distress or trouble.

The bible tells us in Hebrews 11 how so many had faith in the words of God or promises of God and they saw what was promised to them because they believed what God said. You must get so full of God's word on the thing you are seeking him for that you are convinced that it is going to happen for you. You've got to get in the word of God until you "know in your knower" as Dr. Hoffman would say. Some have unbelief because they have no confidence or trust in the word. As a result, they don't have any word, any substance (Heb 11:1) of what they are hoping for and subsequently fail to see what they are (diligently) seeking Him for.

So, you must get into the word of God

and see what God says about your healing, your prosperity, your life, your health, your children, and about you and your identity. Continue in God's word and prayer until you are convinced of His word, and it fills your spirit. Then it will become a reality and you will see exactly what God said. God's word is filled with covenants He made with His people.

All you have to do is open the bible, study look at the covenants, and believe exactly what He promised.

CHAPTER 6:
COVENANTS

From the beginning God is revealed as the covenant maker. Covenant can be simply defined as a strong binding agreement that is formed between two or more people. A basic meaning of "covenant" in the Bible is summed up in the words of Jeremiah in chapter 31 verse 33: *"I will be their God; and they will be my people."* God enters into a special relationship with men and women. He commits himself to protect His people, and in return he expects obedience from them.

Most covenants in the Bible are between

God and man. There are also "man to man" covenants in the Old Testament. The Bible itself is arranged into two major covenants: the Old and the New. They are more often called the Old and New Testaments (which means the same thing). The Old Covenant is the one made with Moses on Mt. Sinai, when the Ten Commandments were given to God's people as the basic rules for living. This covenant forms the basis for Israel's religion.

There are also other covenants in the Old Testament. There is the one God made with Noah after the flood. This is God's general covenant with all people. Then there is the covenant God made with Abraham. God promised that his descendants would have a land of their own, and he urged them to share their blessings with the other nations of the earth. This is God's covenant with His special people, renewed in the covenant with Moses at Mt. Sinai.

The New Testament writers show that the New Covenant between God and men, to which the Old Testament looks forward, rests on the death of Jesus. Jesus Himself said "this cup of the New Covenant, sealed with My blood." The book of Hebrews compares the Old and New Covenants. The New Covenant offers something that the Old could never secure-release from the power of sin, and the freedom to obey God.

Scriptures that detail convents God made with His people.

Genesis 9:1-17; 1 And God blessed Noah and his sons and said to them, "Be fruitful and multiply, and fill the earth.

2 "The fear of you and the terror of you will be on every beast of the earth and on every bird of the sky; with everything that creeps on the ground, and all the fish of the sea, into your hand they are given.

3 "Every moving thing that is alive shall be food for you; I give all to you, as I gave the green plant.

4 "Only you shall not eat flesh with its life, that is, its blood.

5 "Surely I will require your lifeblood; from every beast I will require it. And from every man, from every man's brother I will require the life of man.

6 "Whoever sheds man's blood, By man his blood shall be shed, For in the image of God He made man.

7 "As for you, be fruitful and multiply; Populate the earth abundantly and multiply in it."

8 Then God spoke to Noah and to his sons with him, saying,

9 "Now behold, I Myself do establish My covenant with you, and with your descendants after you;

10 and with every living creature that is with you, the birds, the cattle, and every beast of the earth with you; of all that comes out of the ark, even every beast of the earth.

11 "I establish My covenant with you; and all flesh shall never again be cut off by the water of the flood, neither shall there again be a flood to destroy the earth."

12 God said, "This is the sign of the covenant which I am making between Me and you and every living creature that is with you, for all successive generations;

13 I set My bow in the cloud, and it shall be for a sign of a covenant between Me and the earth.

14 "It shall come about, when I bring a cloud over the earth, that the bow will be seen in the cloud,

15 and I will remember My covenant, which is between Me and you and every living creature of all flesh; and never again shall the water become a flood to destroy all flesh.

16 "When the bow is in the cloud, then I will look upon it, to remember the everlasting covenant between God and every living creature of all flesh that is on the earth."

17 And God said to Noah, "This is the sign

of the covenant which I have established between Me and all flesh

Genesis 12:1-3; 1 Now the Lord said to Abram, "Go forth from your country, And from your relatives And from your father's house, To the land which I will show you;

2 And I will make you a great nation, And I will bless you, And make your name great; And so you shall be a blessing;

3 And I will bless those who bless you, And the one who curses you I will curse. And in you all the families of the earth will be blessed."

Genesis 15:17-21; 17 It came about when the sun had set, that it was very dark, and behold, there appeared a smoking oven and a flaming torch which passed between these pieces.

18 On that day the Lord made a covenant

with Abram, saying, "To your descendants I have given this land, From the river of Egypt as far as the great river, the river Euphrates:

19 the Kenite and the Kenizzite and the Kadmonite

20 and the Hittite and the Perizzite and the Rephaim

21 and the Amorite and the Canaanite and the Girgashite and the Jebusite."

Exodus 19:6; 6 and you shall be to Me a kingdom of priests and a holy nation.' These are the words that you shall speak to the sons of Israel."

Exodus 20:1-7; 1 Then God spoke all these words, saying,

2 "I am the Lord your God, who brought you out of the land of Egypt, out of the house of slavery.

3 "You shall have no other gods before Me.

4 "You shall not make for yourself an idol, or any likeness of what is in heaven above or on the earth beneath or in the water under the earth.

5 "You shall not worship them or serve them; for I, the Lord your God, am a jealous God, visiting the iniquity of the fathers on the children, on the third and the fourth generations of those who hate Me,

6 but showing lovingkindness to thousands, to those who love Me and keep My commandments.

7 "You shall not take the name of the Lord your God in vain, for the Lord will not leave him unpunished who takes His name in vain.

I Corinthians 11:23-25; 23 For I received from the Lord that which I also delivered to you, that the Lord Jesus in the night in which He was betrayed took bread;

24 and when He had given thanks, He broke it and said, "This is My body, which is for you; do this in remembrance of Me."

25 In the same way He took the cup also after supper, saying, "This cup is the new covenant in My blood; do this, as often as you drink it, in remembrance of Me."

26 For as often as you eat this bread and drink the cup, you proclaim the Lord's death until He comes.

Hebrews 8:7-13; 7 For if that first covenant had been faultless, there would have been no occasion sought for a second.

8 For finding fault with them, He says, "Behold, days are coming, says the Lord,

When I will effect a new covenant With the house of Israel and with the house of Judah;

9 Not like the covenant which I made with their fathers on the day when I took them by the hand To lead them out of the land of Egypt; For they did not continue in My covenant, And I did not care for them, says the Lord.

10 "For this is the covenant that I will make with the house of Israel After those days, says the Lord: I will put My laws into their minds, And I will write them on their hearts. And I will be their God, And they shall be My people.

11 "And they shall not teach everyone his fellow citizen, And everyone his brother, saying, 'Know the Lord,' For all will know Me, From the least to the greatest of them.

12 "For I will be merciful to their

iniquities, And I will remember their sins no more."

13 When He said, "A new covenant," He has made the first obsolete. But whatever is becoming obsolete and growing old is ready to disappear.

Hebrews 10:1-10; 1 For the Law, since it has only a shadow of the good things to come and not the very form of things, can never, by the same sacrifices which they offer continually year by year, make perfect those who draw near.

2 Otherwise, would they not have ceased to be offered, because the worshipers, having once been cleansed, would no longer have had consciousness of sins?

3 But in those sacrifices there is a reminder of sins year by year.

4 For it is impossible for the blood of bulls

and goats to take away sins.

5 Therefore, when He comes into the world, He says, "Sacrifice and offering You have not desired, But a body You have prepared for Me;

6 In whole burnt offerings and sacrifices for sin You have taken no pleasure.

7 "Then I said, 'Behold, I have come (In the scroll of the book it is written of Me) To do Your will, O God.'"

8 After saying above, "Sacrifices and offerings and whole burnt offerings and sacrifices for sin You have not desired, nor have You taken pleasure in them" (which are offered according to the Law),

9 then He said, "Behold, I have come to do Your will." He takes away the first in order to establish the second.

10 By this will we have been sanctified

through the offering of the body of Jesus Christ once for all.

CHAPTER 7:
IMPARTATION

If we reflect on many stories in the bible, individuals were often mentored or received greater strength in weaker areas because they were connected to a source that had accomplished where they wanted to be in life. In these covenant relationships, there is a transfer of power from God to empower you to be what you see. We call this impartation.

This new covenant gives us a fresh revelation of the character of God. We not only seek the kingdom of God and His righteousness, but in the Blood we find IT! The model prayers states, "Thy will be done on Earth, as it is in Heaven." Translation: God's will is to bring Heaven to Earth and to do so He makes covenant with man. When men who are in covenant with God get together, they make up the Body of Christ, or the Church, and bring the Kingdom of God on Earth!

"Now it came about when he had finished talking to Saul, that the soul of David and Jonathan were knit together and he loved him as himself. And Saul took him that day and did not let him return to his father's house. Then Jonathan made a covenant with David because he loved him as himself. And Jonathan stripped himself of the robe that was on him and gave it to David, with his armor, including his sword and his bow and his belt. **(I Samuel 18:1-4 NASV).**

Boy! What a covenant between two God fearing men. They became unified and agreed to the point that Jonathan took down his defense and joined himself to David. He took his armor off, thus opening himself up to receive whatever David would return to him. David returned love. The armor was the token of exchange which was common among covenant makers in the Bible. God gives protection and provision and we are to respond in loving obedience. In giving David his royal robe, his armor and his sword, his bow and belt, Jonathan was giving to David, his authority of succession to his father's throne. To impart means to give, share, distribute, grant. The word implies liberality or generosity. It is used to exhort those with two outer tunics to give one to someone who has not (Luke 3:11); to encourage people to give with cheerful outflow (Romans 12:8); and to urge workers to labor with industry, in order to give to him who has a need (Ephesians 4:28). Ephesians 4:7-8 says, *"But unto every one of us is given grace according to the measure of the gift of Christ. Wherefore he saith, when he ascended up on high, he led captivity captive, and gave gifts unto men."* Therefore, every Christian has a gift in God. Verse (12) says, *".... for the work of the ministry, for the edifying of the Body of Christ."*

Writing to the church at Rome, Paul says... "For I long to see you, that I may impart unto you some spiritual gift, to the end that ye may be established" (Romans 1:11). Here, to impart means to simply "to give over and to share." It means to convey from one person to another. The apostle Paul had the desire to impart to the saints some spiritual gift or spiritual help. Spiritual impartations are given to help us fulfill the will of God for our lives. This is part of the equipping. We are equipped to do the work of the ministry through impartation. The result is establishment. The New English Bible says, "to make you strong."

The Twentieth Century New Testament says "and so give you fresh strength." Believers are equipped with fresh strength as a result of impartation. Impartation will come often through association. In this way, there will be a transference of anointing from or to the people you associate with. We can receive through impartation from the ministries we submit to and associate with. There are certain people whom I believe the Lord has destined you to hook up with in the Spirit. They will have the spiritual deposits you need. It is not the will of God that we lack any necessary gift, information, materials, or anointing (in manifestation of the Holy Spirit). He has given us the means to obtain all we need. He is ready and willing to equip us with all the grace we need to complete our commission which is to preach the gospel to all nations and make disciples of men.

If we are lacking, it's not God's fault. It is important to associate with strong churches and strong ministries. If you associate yourself with weakness, you will become weak. If you associate with strength, you will become strong. You will become like the people you associate with. Don't allow yourself to become weak by linking up with the wrong kind of people. "And God wrought special miracles by the hands of Paul; So that from his body were brought unto the sick handkerchief's or aprons, and the disease departed from them, and evil spirits went out of them" (Acts 19:11-12). Here once again an object was exchanged (Paul's materials), as a point of contact (tokens of covenant) to the other person who was involved in the impartation.

When seeking God for an understanding of who He has called you to be, you must join or connect with someone who has a revelation of who God has made them to be. Strength begets strength. Through divine connection, God can also impart to you through the anointing on that person's life to be who He has made you to be. I have found this to be true even in my life. When I was seeking God to get a real understanding of who He made me to be according to His word, I got serious about my walk with Him. Started talking with someone who had overcome in the area of who they were. Through that divine connection, through impartation from that minister to me, I was able to get a true revelation of who God designed me to be. We can never do these things alone; it takes Godly covenant prayer partners to get what we need from God. It goes back to unity (as we spoke about in Chapter 3). That unity in prayer with someone who has overcome in that area will cause an impartation to take place and you can freely receive exactly what you are seeking from God. You are never alone so do not walk alone. God has appointed someone to walk alongside you and impart strength to you where you are weak. By faith, let us walk together on this journey.

CHAPTER 8:
UNDERSTANDING REDEMPTION

In order to boldly come before God in prayer for what we need, we have to get a real understanding of what God did for us through Jesus. Many are held from understanding who God made them to be because of shame and guilt of their past. Your do not have to live life feeling anything but victorious once you accept what God did for you so long ago. Freedom is awaiting your reception of what God did for you through Christ. By getting a real understanding here, God is able to establish us in faith according to the plan of redemption which had been hidden over the ages. After the Fall in the Garden of Eden, God spoke and outlined the plan. What He laid down put Satan out of business completely. Praise God! He has commanded that the plan of redemption be revealed to His people by His Word. This outline will help you, step by step, understand the reality of it and prevent Satan from lording over you.

1. The Plan of Redemption called for an Incarnation (The Union of Divinity with Humanity in Jesus Christ). Man was the key figure in the Fall. Therefore, it took a man, Jesus, to be the key figure in the redemption of man. When we were born into this world, ruled by Satan, we did not naturally know God. Therefore, the objective of the incarnation is that men may be given the right to become sons of God by receiving the nature of God (John 1:12-13; II Peter 1:3-4).

2. Redemption Comes From Knowledge.

God's divine power has already provided everything that pertains to life and godliness. You can escape from the corruption in the world and partake of the divine nature of God. And you can have peace and grace multiplied to you through the knowledge of God and of Jesus our Lord (I Peter 1:1-4). It's there for you! But this revelation knowledge is not sense knowledge, doctrine, philosophies and creeds. It is the reality and full truth of the Word of God revealed by the Holy Spirit (James 3:13-18). Revelation knowledge is literally knowledge brought to you by revelation!

3. Satan's Lordship Has Been Broken. Revelation 12:11 tells us that the believers overcome by the blood of the lamb and by the word of their testimony, or confession. Confession brings possession. Boldly confess, "I am an overcomer by the blood of the Lamb and by the word of my testimony. I am redeemed from the lordship of Satan. I can stop his assignments every time." (II Corinthians 10:4; James 4:7). Satan is not the head of the Church. Jesus is the Head of the Church (Ephesians 4:15-16, 5:23; Colossians 1:18, 2:10). Satan has no rule over you. Hallelujah!

4.   You Are Bought With A Price.   I Corinthians 6:19-20 tells us we are the temple of the Holy Spirit, which is received from God. This means that we don't own ourselves. We were bought with a price paid through the plan of redemption. Because of that, we should glorify God in our bodies and spirits.

5. God's Response. When you begin to take your place and assume your rights and privileges in Christ, then God begins to respond to you. The Word gives us our inheritance (Acts 20:32; Colossians 1:12). As you study the scriptures in this outline, our prayer is that you come to the full knowledge of who you are in Christ, especially in light of the redemption plan. God will bless you! Amen!

Once you understand your redemption and what Christ did for you, you can stand against anything Satan may try and bring your way. Because God gave His only son to die for you and paid the penalty of every sin you could ever commit, you can walk with confidence because you know that you are forgiven, and you are now a part of a new family. Our Father in heaven is not sick so you do not have to be sick, our Father is not trying to find who He is, so you do not have to suffer any longer in that way. All we must do is get in His word, receive what He said, confess exactly what He said, then see what He said.

CHAPTER 9:
UNDERSTANDING CONFESSION

Ask yourself, what have I been saying when it comes to who I am. Think about the last words that you said about yourself. Were they negative or positive? Did they bring you understanding or more confusion? Well let me tell you this, words are spiritual, they carry power. The words we speak are of vital importance to our lives. Jesus said, *"I say unto you, that every idle word that men shall speak, they shall give account thereof in the day of judgment. For by thy words thou shalt be justified, and by thy words thou shalt be condemned"* (**Matthew 12:36-37**).

When God created the human race, he placed in us the special ability to choose our own words and speak them forth at will. That ability makes the human being different from all other creatures, even the angels. Angels can speak but they can only speak the words God tells them to speak. They act, but only by the command of God. Man's unique ability to choose and speak words has become a key factor in the development of the human race. Proverbs 12:14 tells us that we shall be satisfied with good by the fruit of our mouths. In Matthew 12:34, Jesus said, "...*out of the abundance of the heart the mouth speaketh.*"

If we are not enjoying the reality of God's Word, it is because our confession has us bound. Confession of the Word of God isn't lying, for what we must realize is that we are not trying to get God to do anything. The benefits God has given us in His Word are ours already and Satan is trying to steal them!

So confessing isn't lying. It's a statement of truth. If you didn't know Jesus bore your sickness and disease and told someone you were healed because of your own merits, then you would be lying. But to tell someone that you are healed because the Bible says "by His stripes you were healed," is speaking the truth that Jesus has already redeemed you from the curse of the law (Deuteronomy 28; Galatians 3:13).

Here are five basic confessions for you to use so that you can enjoy all that God has for you:

1. **Jesus is My Lord**. Philippians 2:9-11

"I confess the complete lordship of Jesus Christ. Jesus is Lord over all and He has given me authority. As I confess Him, His Word and His Na6 me, and resist Satan in His Name, Satan must bow His knee."

2. **I Do Not Have A Care**. I Peter 5:7; Psalms 37:23-24

"I cast all my care on Jesus because He cares for me. He upholds me as He guides my steps."

3. **I Do Not Want.** Psalms 23:1; Philip 4:19

"The Lord is my Shepherd. I shall not want. For my God supplies all my need according to His riches in glory by Christ Jesus.

4. **I Am Free From Sin, Sickness, Sorrow, Grief and Fear.** Isaiah 53:3-5; Matthew 8:17; I Peter 2:24

"Every sin, sickness, disease, sorrow and grief was laid on Jesus so that I could be free from them. Therefore, today I am forgiven, healed, healthy and well. I live in divine health."

5. **Jesus is made unto me Wisdom, Righteousness, Sanctification and**

Redemption.

I Corinthians 1:30; Colossians 2:10

"I confess that Jesus is my wisdom, righteousness, sanctification, and redemption. Only in Him am I entirely complete."

Continue to change your circumstances by filling your heart with the Word of God. Confess these truths and other scriptures so that the words that come out of your mouth are life-changing words. Let your word be God's word! So, instead of repeating those negative words or confessions about who you are, say what God says about you in His word. Let that be your confession. When you feel you are going to say something that is contrary to what God has said about you, open His word and confess what He says. Keep practicing this until God's word about you fills your heart and spirit and becomes who you are.

CHAPTER 10:
CONFESSIONS/PRAYERS

It is important to say what God says about who you are. If we are not careful, we can pick up a fabricated identity about ourselves from the world around us. It is so easy when you are searching for who you are to pick up an image or perspective of who you are or want to be from watching our favorite shows, commercials, social media, etc. And from those images we can sometimes craft a perception of ourselves that may not reflect who we truly are, but it may appeal to us. I can say from experience no amount of makeup, no outfit, or any other thing but understanding who you are from God's perspective is going to give you the greatest fulfilment.

God has crafted us all with a distinctive reason in mind. His word is filled with descriptions of who we are. For us to get a true understanding of who we are, we must get into His word and say what He said about us.

You must pray and confess God's word to see what God sees about you. Here are some scriptures that describe who we are in Christ.

- **Loved:** Galatians 2:20 ESV--I have been crucified with Christ. It is no longer I who live, but Christ who lives in me. And the life I now live in the flesh I live by faith in the Son of God, who loved me and gave himself for me.

- **Belong to God:** 1 Corinthians 6:20 ESV- for you were bought with a price. So glorify God in your body.

  Romans 8:16 ESV- The Spirit himself bears witness with our spirit that we are children of God,

  Galatians 3:26 ESV- for in Christ Jesus you are all sons of God, through faith.

- **In Christ:** 1 John 4:4 ESV- Little children, you are from God and have overcome them, for he who is in you is greater than he who is in the world.

  Philippians 3:20 ESV- But our citizenship is in heaven, and from it we await a Savior, the Lord Jesus Christ,

  1 Corinthians 12:27 ESV- Now you are the body of Christ and individually members of it.

  1 Corinthians 6:17 ESV- But he who is joined to the Lord becomes one spirit with him.

- **Created By God:** Ephesians 2:10 ESV-
  For we are his workmanship, created in
  Christ Jesus for good works, which God
  prepared beforehand, that we should
  walk in them.
- **Children of God:** John 1:12 ESV- But to
  all who did receive him, who believed in
  his name, he gave the right to become
  children of God,
  Galatians 3:26 ESV- For in Christ Jesus
  you are all sons of God, through faith.
  Romans 8:17 ESV- And if children, then
  heirs—heirs of God and fellow heirs with
  Christ, provided we suffer with him in
  order that we may also be glorified with
  him.
- **Forgiven/Redeemed By God:** Romans
  6:6 ESV- We know that our old self was
  crucified with him in order that the body
  of sin might be brought to nothing, so

that we would no longer be enslaved to sin.

Romans 8:1 ESV- There is therefore now no condemnation for those who are in Christ Jesus.

Ephesians 1:7 ESV - In him we have redemption through his blood, the forgiveness of our trespasses, according to the riches of his grace,

- **Chosen by God:** 1 Thessalonians 1:4 ESV- For we know, brothers loved by God, that he has chosen you,

  1 Peter 2:9 ESV- But you are a chosen race, a royal priesthood, a holy nation, a people for his own possession, that you may proclaim the excellencies of him who called you out of darkness into his marvelous light.

- **Ambassadors for God:** 2 Corinthians 5:20-Therefore, we are ambassadors for Christ, God making his appeal through us. We implore you on behalf of Christ, be reconciled to God.

- **Empowered by God:** Philippians 4:13 ESV- I can do all things through him who strengthens me.

  Ephesians 1:3 ESV- Blessed be the God and Father of our Lord Jesus Christ, who has blessed us in Christ with every spiritual blessing in the heavenly places, Romans 8:37 ESV- No, in all these things we are more than conquerors through him who loved us.

- **Protected by God:** 1 John 5:18 ESV- We know that everyone who has been born of God does not keep on sinning, but he who was born of God protects him, and the evil one does not touch him.

- **Provided for by God:** Philippians 4:19 ESV-And my God will supply every need of yours according to his riches in glory in Christ Jesus.

- **God dwells in you:** 1 Corinthians 3:16 ESV- Do you not know that you are God's temple and that God's Spirit dwells in you?

Prayers For The World Around Us

A Prayer For Our Government

I Timothy 2:1-2 says that we are to pray, intercede and give thanks for the kings and all people in authority. This is God's command to every believer today. Here is a confession for you to use in prayer for our nation and its leaders. Pray it in faith, believing, and remember God watches over His Word to perform it. (Jeremiah 1:12, The Amplified Bible)

"Father, in Jesus' Name, I give thanks for our country and its government. I bring before You the men and women in positions of authority.

I pray and intercede for the president, congressmen, senators, judges, policemen, governors, mayors of our land.

I pray for all people in authority over us in any

way.

I pray that the Spirit of the Lord rests upon them. I believe that skillful and godly wisdom has entered into the heart of our president and knowledge is pleasant to him. Discretion watches over him; understanding keeps him and delivers him from the way of evil and from evil men.

Father, I ask You to encompass the president with men and women who make their hearts and ears attentive to godly counsel and who do that which is right in Your sight.

I believe You cause them to be men and women of integrity, who are obedient concerning us. I believe that they lead us in a quiet and peaceable life in all godliness and honesty.

Your Word declares, "Blessed is the nation

whose God is the Lord." I receive Your Blessing and declare with my mouth that Your people dwell safely in this land and they prosper abundantly.

It is written in Your Word that the heart of the king is in the hand of the Lord and that You turn it whichever way You desire. I believe the heart of our leader is in Your hand and that his decisions are divinely directed of the Lord. I give thanks unto You that the good news of the gospel is published in our land. The Word of the Lord prevails and grows mightily in the hearts and lives of the people. I give thanks for this land and the leaders you have given to us, in Jesus' Name. I proclaim that Jesus is Lord over the United States of America!

Prayer Reference: I Timothy 2:1-2; Proverbs 2:11-12, The Amplified Bible; Psalms 33:12; Proverbs 21:1

A Prayer For Our Schools

More than 44 million students are enrolled in the United States' public schools. They are instructed by 2.6 million teachers.

* These numbers certainly justify a tremendous spiritual outreach and call to intercessory prayer. What are we contending for? he souls, the lives and the futures of the upcoming generations. Today's educational system had drastically separated from what God first established in this nation through leaders who sought His counsel. The Word of God once served as the basic element in educating Americans. The Ten Commandments were even displayed in schools as a guide to moral attitude and conduct. The state of our educational system may look hopeless, but when something looks hopeless, it is evidence of a spiritual problem. Hope can begin to work in these

circumstances. Hope is a spiritual force which grows stronger and stronger the longer we stand. Faith can begin to work in these circumstances. "Now faith is the substance of things, hoped for, the evidence of things not seen" (Hebrews 11:1). Patience can begin to work in these circumstances. The definition of patience is being constant or being the same at all times. As believers exercise these three spiritual forces, the Word of God can work to change the direction of American education. Our God is a good God! He caused the captivity of Judah and Israel to be reversed, then rebuilt them as they were at first (Jeremiah 33:7). He can do the same in our schools. Pray this prayer of faith and set yourself in agreement with the Word of God for the restoration of God's principles in all levels of education.

"Almighty God, I set myself in agreement with the Word of God and with what You once established in American education. I release my hope and faith in your Word.

I patiently expect Your Glory to be manifest in schools all across our nation. I come before You on behalf of the students, educators, and administrators of the entire educational system in America. Lord Jesus, I ask you to restore honor, integrity, virtue, and peace in American classrooms. I confess Isaiah 54:13: 'All thy children shall be taught of the Lord; and great shall be the peace of thy children.' Every time I hear a report of violence and terror in our schools, I will say out loud, "Our children are taught of the Lord and great is the peace and the Anointing upon them!" Jesus, You and I know the educators and the administrators cannot teach and run our schools without You and Your Anointing. So, I intercede and give thanks for those You have ordained and placed in positions of authority and responsibility in our schools across

America. I believe for Your Anointing to be in them and upon them.

I am not waiting until I see the Spirit of God moving in this situation. I am starting my confession NOW! I combine my faith with those who are praying and believing for the wisdom, and honor, power, and Glory of God to be demonstrated in our school system. I am releasing my faith for the next generation! Lord Jesus, I thank You for the redemptive work You are doing in our schools and in the people who run them.

The students and teachers are on Your heart and they are on mine, too. Our schools will be a joy, a praise and a glory before all the nations of the earth! Nations will fear God and tremble because of all the goodness, peace, prosperity, security and stability You have provided in Jesus!" *National Center for Education Statistics Report, May 1996

A Prayer For Revival

Waves of revival have swept around the world in the 20th Century. Today, the five largest churches in the world are Spirit-filled and growing daily. Pentecostals are increasing in great numbers as worldwide revival brings the life of God to the church and to all mankind. The Hebrew word for revive is chayah which means to live, have life, remain alive, sustain life, nourish, and preserve life, live prosperously, live forever, be quickened, be alive, be restored to life and health.

According to that definition, revival is not just a one-time shot of life. Revival is a continual nourishment, preservation, quickening and restoration to life. Revival begins when people return to God. It breaks forth from intercessory prayer and continues when people repent and no longer tolerate sin in their lives.

After Jesus ascended to heaven, the disciples returned to the upper room and continued in daily prayer, in one accord, and in one place. Then, at the appointed time, the Holy Spirit burst onto the scene with the sound of a mighty rushing wind. Peter and the others received God's long-awaited promise of the Holy Spirit's anointing. Acts 2:17-19 repeats the prophecy of Joel, "And it shall come to pass in the last days, says God, That I will pour out my spirit in those days, And they shall prophesy... I will show wonders in heaven above and signs in the earth beneath..." (New King James Version).

As they moved out into the streets from the upper room, men from every part of the world saw and heard something different. Peter's great sermon, preached under the anointing of God, brought understanding, conviction of sin and the life of God to those who heard and responded in faith. Prayer, the anointed preaching of the Word, and a supernatural move of God all working together brought revival-God's life-giving power.

Oh, what a time to live in! Destruction and despair may be on one hand, but revival and miracles are on the other. Revival is spontaneous and ongoing. It happens when the Spirit of God moves among the people. God never intended for the Pentecostal revival to stop. That is why it is so important to be ready and available as God moves and pours our His Spirit. He can minister life at any moment, to one or to a multitude, to a person in a barren wilderness or to many people in a crowded city.

Revival happens whenever the Word of God prevails. Miracles, signs, and wonders happen wherever the Word of God prevails. Hearts and lives are changed wherever the Word of

God prevails. The Bible says …God working with them and confirming His word with signs following (Mark 16:20).

Look in the Word of God, which is life to them, revival will come and remain. Revival will become an ongoing way of life. As you set yourself in agreement with God's will for revival, pray the following prayer or one similar, expecting God to move.

"Father God, because you care for Your people and want all mankind to have life, You desire revival. Your revival brings life and nourishment, preservation and restoration. Thank you for sending Jesus to give us Your abundant life Lord, start a revival in me first. I am Your servant and I place myself in position to receive revival. I feed on the Scriptures as a sheep feeds in green pastures, because Your words are life to me.

Holy Spirit of God, You raised Jesus from

the dead and You dwell in me. So, I yield to You to energize my spirit, restore my soul, and rejuvenate my mortal body. I renew my mind with Your Word. In my innermost being is a well of living water and I am revived! Revival not only is life to me, but life to everyone who calls on the Name of the Lord. Therefore, I intercede on behalf of the people. I call upon You as the God of Abraham, Isaac, and Jacob I call upon the mighty Name of Jesus. All of mankind needs life, Lord! All of mankind needs revival because it is life- Your life. I speak and sow seeds of revival everywhere I go. I send forth angels to reap the harvest of revival all over the world. I put my hand to the sickle to reap the rich harvest of revival in my home, my church, my community, in the marketplace, on the job, in my country and in all the world. Pour Yourself out on the people. Lord of the harvest, send forth laborers, positioning them in strategic places to minister as You pour out Your Spirit on all flesh. Almighty God, show Yourself mighty and strong with signs and wonders. Holy Spirit breathe on all the people of the world. I pray this in the Name above all names, Jesus. Amen."

Prayer references: John 3:16-17, 10:10; Proverbs 4:20-22; John 6:63; Romans 8:11; Ephesians 4:23-24; Colossians 3:10; John 4:14, 7:38; Matthew 13:39, 9:38; II Chronicles 16:9; Romans 15:19

CHAPTER 11:
YOU ARE UNDERSTOOD

Hey ladies, I am going to be totally real with you. I have been in your shoes. I have felt the feeling and emotions that come with wandering and feeling lost when it comes to understanding who you are and what you are to do with your life. Many begin to feel this around their teenage years and yes, that is when it hit me the hardest. I felt trapped in my own world and very alone. I had no complete concept of what I wanted to do with myself, however, I knew I loved fashion. I had so much potential but no way to draw on it to even began to get an idea of who I was. Still searching for an image or idea that I could call me, I filled my head with popular music, reality shows, YouTube, and so on. I could not even begin to express the amount of money I spent on purchasing clothing, hair products, and makeup, just to get the look or image I saw. I kept fixing the outside but did not even change what the real issue was- me!

The discovering of who God called me to be happened in an unlikely way. After moving to an area where I did not have access to the fashion stores I used to shop at to get my beauty regimen and treatments, I was forced take a hard look at myself. I had to change. Without all of the fluff and no way to build the facade that I once kept building, I had to face myself and deal with the issues I had in life. It was through hearing and reading the word, prayer, and fellowship with other like-minded believers that I began to see who God called me to be.

I was taught the word, so I knew right from wrong, I knew the truth, but I still was undecided as to whether I wanted to live the saved life that I grew up seeing. See, the world makes you feel that it is boring and uncool to live for Christ but it is quite the opposite. In Christ, there is nothing but life, which includes love, peace, unexplainable joy, and so many good things. On the other hand, the world's way only permits or leads to one thing, death. While straddling the fence, my mind began to wander and the feeling of being lost began to grow even bigger. However, my life began to change when I made a quality decision. A decision to be in Christ and fellowship with His people. I choose to follow the path that God had me on and not straddle or wander any more. I began to talk to God again, read His word, and not forsake or disregard assembling with His people.

Through my connection with the body of Christ, or partnership, my whole life changed. When I was trying to join in with the world and their concepts, I could not fit in or find my identity which left me unfulfilled and feeling alone.

The key here is that I felt alone. When you are called by God you cannot and will not fit in with the worldly crowd. You will feel out of place and alone when you try to join a club you do not belong in. I Peter 1:9 says that you are a "peculiar people a royal priesthood." When you have accepted Christ into your life, you may sometimes seem strange, weird, or abnormal to those who have chosen the worldly way of living. However, when you have accepted Christ, we are to fellowship with His people. In that you will see you are not alone as I discovered. Instead, you will feel complete acceptance. I was never alone, I had a great family and church family that cared for me. That feeling of loneliness comes when one drifts from their covering. A wolf can only capture a sheep when they drift away and isolate themselves from the fold. The key that solved my wandering and drifting was **partnership.** Partnership comes from the same word as fellowship. It is the coming together of two or more parties that share a common interest. It says in Matthew 18:20 that where two or three are gathered together in His name, He is in the midst of them. So, as we partner with a prayer base of believers, we can get answers as we pray and understand who he has made us to be.

CHAPTER 12:
YOUR OPPORTUNITY TO PARTNER

We discussed earlier in the book about a woman named Lydia. After learning about Christ, receiving Him and getting a better understanding of who she was, Lydia immediately sought for a way to partner with Paul in an effort to reach others. She opened her house to Paul and those with him. Lydia's house became the first church in Europe, which is known as the Philippian church. The Philippian church is noted in the bible because of their partnership with Paul in the gospel.

As the Apostle Paul said, *"I thank my God*

upon every remembrance of you... For your fellowship in the gospel from the first day until now... because I have you in my heart; inasmuch as both in my bonds, and in the defense and confirmation of the gospel, ye are all partakers of my grace (Philippians 1:3, 5,7)." Paul was saying "I have you in my heart, I'm praying for you and I'm not going to let you fail!" His partners had become a major part of his ministry. They fought alongside him in prayer, they ministered to his needs, and provided for other ministers that he sent to help build them spiritually. That's how partnership works.

The Partners have a significant role in this ministry. God provides for the ministry through them- through their prayers, words of encouragement and support, and through their giving to what God is doing through the ministry. And every day we see and hear of the great rewards they are receiving as a result of their partnership. If God is directing you to become a Partner, or if you are already a Partner, press in to get a revelation of God's will for you, and then get ready for the adventure and rewards that come when you release the power of partnership in your life.

CHAPTER 13:
THE BLESSING OF THE TWICE SOWN SEED

"And he...took the five loaves, and two fishes, and looking up toward heaven he blessed, and brake, and gave the loaves to his disciples, and the disciples to the multitude. And they did all eat, and were filled: and they took up of the fragments that remained twelve baskets full. And they that had eaten were about five thousand men beside women and children" **(Matthew 14:19-21)**.

Sowing into A.D Long Ministries, an

auxiliary of FOFMI, stretches further than the hundreds of lives it touches. It stretches from orphanages to healing ministries to evangelical meetings to medical teams. We reach all over the globe through the principle of the twice sown seed.

When you give to A.D Long Ministries, 10 percent of every gift is given to other ministries that reach people we can't. We actually re-sow a tenth of your gift and product purchase into lives all over the world. And just like the boy who gave his loaves and fish to Jesus, we see the increase on the seed-faith gifts of our partners. Through partnership in ministry, we are reaching greater numbers of people than any of us could reach on our own- people who have no other way to hear the good news.

We stand with ministries which train and minister through educating, credentialing and assisting men and women in the Word of God, prayer, and divine leadership. We support outreaches which conduct yearly ministerial conferences in several countries, providing Bibles in English and other native languages to equip Pastors to win the lost to Christ...a tremendous need! Providing theological training and books for Pastors and ministers, developing Bible schools, helping the children, feeding the poor, promoting soul winning and reaching the lost and church planting. We promote the gospel through broadcasting Gospel and Christian music as well as local, national, and international ministers on www.WVIU.net. We give into other ministries that teach local ministers by the hundreds every year in Guatemala, send evangelistic teams into the isolated Islands and mountains of the Philippines, and telecast the good news across Eastern Europe.

Orphan children in Haiti, former gang

members in Los Angeles, Bible school students in Italy and troubled girls in Tennessee are all among the millions of lives touched by the love of our partners giving.

In addition, we support locally with children's ministries, volunteer services programs, campus and young adult outreach, medical assistance, job creation, evangelism, continuing education assistance, clothing, food, teaching and preaching.

You enable us to put legs to our prayers by putting substance into our hands to be effective soldiers of the cross. As a result, you will share the reward of this harvest someday! Lives are changed eternally. Blessings overflow to the giver. That's the power of partnership. That's the power of the twice-sown-seed!

A PARTNER............

One who shares responsibility in some common activity with another individual or group. Our Part is to...

- Pray on a daily basis that God's blessing be upon you
- Provide spiritual and life enrichment resources for you online.
- Bless you with a free gift from time to time (such as music or message downloads or other gifts)
- Provide partner conferences, meetings and events online and offline
- Serve Christ through serving mankind
- Provide you with a tuition paid course through Interfaith University (Optional)

Your Responsibility...

- Pray for us always
- Support our outreach efforts especially in your area
- Prayerfully sow financially into our outreach efforts.
- Always uplift us with the words that you speak.
- Serve Christ through serving mankind.

A. D. Long, I want to access the Power of this anointed Prayer Partnership!

My Name is: _____

My Address is: _____

Phone: _____ Age: _____
M ____ F ____

I am writing my prayer request on this form.

Enclosed is my love gift of $ _____.

I am pledging ___ $7 ___$10 ___$20 ___$100 ___$500 ___Other $_____ per month to help you accomplish the vision of winning the lost and encouraging the saints through the Word of God!
_____, Signature

Prayer Request:

_____
_____
_____
_____
_____
_____
_____

A.D. Long Ministries
An Auxiliary of Foundations of Faith
1(833) MY-FOFMI
www.FOFMI.org

OUR PRAYER FOR MINISTRY PARTNERS

Father, in the Name of Jesus, we pray to you on behalf of all of our partners, who pray for us, support our local meetings, sow financially into this ministry, and always uplift the ministry, our leaders and their family with the words that they speak.

Father, we pray that you give our partners a full manifestation of your will for their lives. God even as you made your will for Lydia's life clear as she decided to partner with the work of Apostle Paul, we pray that our partners get that same revelation as they follow this ministry. Thank you that they are no longer wondering or lost in life but God we ask that you make your path for them clear, and you give them confidence to walk in that path right now.

Father, we thank you for our partners and for their service and dedication to serve you. Thank you that they bring forth the fruit of the Spirit: love, joy, peace, long suffering, gentleness, goodness, faith, meekness, and temperance.

Father, thank you that our partners are good ground, that they hear Your Word and understand it, and that the Word bears fruit in their lives. They are like trees planted by rivers of water that bring forth fruit in its season. Their leaf shall not wither, and whatever they do shall prosper.

From the first day we heard of our partners, we have not stopped praying for them, asking you God to give them wise minds and spirits attuned to your will, and that they acquire a thorough understanding of the ways in which you work. We pray that our partners are merciful as you our Father is merciful. We pray that they will judge only as they want to be judged and that they do not condemn and they are not condemned. Our partners forgive others and people forgive them. Thank you, Father, that they give and men will give to them- yes, good measure, pressed down, shaken together, running over will they pour into their laps for whatever measure they use with other people, they will use in their dealings with them.

Father, we ask you to bless our partners with all spiritual blessings in heavenly places and that good will might come to them. Thank you that they are generous and lend freely and that they conduct their affairs with justice. Lord, Your Word says that surely they will never be shaken. We pray that they are righteous and remembered forever. They will have no fear of bad news; their hearts are steadfast, trusting in you.

Lord, we ask that your plans be fulfilled in their lives and we thank you for your mercies on their behalf. In Jesus' name we pray. Amen. Colossians 1:9, Psalm 112:5-9, Jeremiah 29:11

ABOUT THE AUTHOR

While attending college, A.D. Long began to feel a deeper call to ministry. She could relate to the lack of confidence she saw in peers and understand the confusion media and opinions presented for those seeking their destiny. In her pursuit for ways to help, God began to deal with Long about using her vocation of fashion to reach out to others. Through Fashioned For A Cause events, she creates opportunities for women and partners with other outreaches to assist beyond her locality. As an author and businesswomen, Long embraces every opportunity to motivate others to discover their identity through God's word.

"I found myself on a quest, like many, to figure out God's will for me. However, through much prayer, studying the word, and fellowship with other like-minded believers, I found my identity in Christ. I want to help other women do the same." -A.D. Long

To contact A.D. Long for other material, go to www.ADLongBooks.com.

Notes:

Notes:

Notes:

Notes:

Made in the USA
Columbia, SC
09 June 2023

17698786R00063